TO

Ben & Siny

FROM

Angela & Mary & families

simple truths®
Motivational & Inspirational Gifts

"Hope Pure And Simple" © 2007 by Max Lucado.
Published under arrangement with Thomas Nelson, Inc., P. O. Box 141000, Nashville, Tennessee 37214.

Simple Truths
1952 McDowell Road, Suite 300
Naperville, Illinois 60563
800-900-3427

Design: Rich Nickel

Photos:
Nels Akerlund (nelsakerland.com): 132
Simon Butterworth Photography (simonbutterworthphotography.com): 32
Joe Decker: 122
Bruce Heinemann (theartofnature.com): 12, 20, 70, 74, 106, 124, 130, 156
Ken Jenkins (kenjenkins.com): 6, 148
Scott Marquis (photographybymarquis.com): 94
Tom Mathews: 52
Todd and Brad Reed Photography (toddandbradreed.com): 34, 62, 72, 120
Jeff Schultz (AlaskaStock.com): 76
Steve Terrill (terrillphoto.com): 10, 24, 56, 68

Printed and bound in the United States of America

ISBN 978-1-60810-042-2

01 WOZ 11

MAX LUCADO

HOPE

pure and simple

316 thoughts to lift your soul

This volume is joyfully dedicated
to Margaret Mechinus,
celebrating countless phone calls,
sent messages, patient affirmations,
and hard work.
Thank you!

A HOPE THAT IS ...

CHAPTER 1

A
Bright
HOPE

— 1 —

With God, every day matters, every person counts.
And that includes you.

— 2 —

You are valuable ... not because of what you do or what you have done,
but simply because you are.

— 3 —

How wide is God's love? Wide enough for the whole world.

— 4 —

A problem is no more a challenge to God
than a twig is to an elephant.

— 5 —

Sow seeds of hope and enjoy optimism.
Sow seeds of doubt and expect insecurity.

— 6 —

God's efforts are strongest when our efforts are useless.

— 7 —

If God can make a billion galaxies, can't he make good out of our bad
and sense out of our faltering lives? Of course he can. He is God.

— 8 —

God is the shepherd who guides, the Lord who provides,
the voice who brings peace in the storm.

— 9 —

God speaks all languages—including yours.

— 10 —

Heaven invites you to set the lens of your heart on the heart of the
Savior and make him the object of your life.

— 11 —

The love of people often increases with performance and decreases
with mistakes. Not so with God's love.

— 12 —

We forget that "impossible" is one of God's favorite words.

I PRAY ALSO THAT THE EYES OF YOUR HEART MAY BE ENLIGHTENED IN ORDER THAT YOU MAY KNOW THE HOPE TO WHICH HE HAS CALLED YOU.

EPHESIANS 1:18 NIV

— 13 —

God loves you with an unearthly love. You can't win it by being winsome. You can't lose it by being a loser.

— 14 —

Does your self-esteem ever sag?
When it does, remember what you are worth,

— 15 —

God—our Shepherd—doesn't check the weather; he makes it.

— 16 —

The Christ of the galaxies is the Christ of your Mondays.
You have a friend in high places.

— 17 —

Want to see a miracle? Plant a word of love heartdeep in a person's life.
Nurture it with a smile and a prayer, and watch what happens.

— 18 —

One of the sweetest reasons God saved you is because he is fond of you.
He likes having you around.

— 19 —

God can live anywhere in the universe, and He chose your heart.
Face it, friend. He's crazy about you.

— 20 —

It's time to let God's love cover all things in your life.
All secrets. All hurts.

— 21 —

You aren't an accident. You aren't an assembly-line product.
You were deliberately planned, specifically gifted, and lovingly
positioned on this earth by the Master Craftsman.

— 22 —

God always rejoices when we dare to dream,

— 23 —

Forgiveness is not saying the one who hurt you was right.
Forgiveness is stating that God is faithful and He will do what is right.

— 24 —

God rested after six days of work, and the world didn't collapse.
What makes us think it will if we do?

$\mathcal{Y}$OU WERE BOUGHT,

NOT WITH SOMETHING THAT RUINS LIKE

GOLD OR SILVER, BUT WITH THE PRECIOUS

BLOOD OF CHRIST, WHO WAS LIKE A

PURE AND PERFECT LAMB.

———

I PETER. 1:18-19

— 25 —

God is greater than our weakness. In fact,
our weakness reveals how great God is.

— 26 —

God knows you better than you know you and has reached
His verdict: He loves you still.

— 27 —

The life of Jesus Christ is a message of hope, a message of mercy,
a message of life in a dark world.

— 28 —

God offers you the possibility of a worry-free life.
Not just less worry, but *no* worry.

— 29 —

God forgives your faults. Why don't you do the same?

— 30 —

God leads us. He will do the right thing at the right time.

— 31 —

If you think God's love for you would be stronger if your faith were, you
are wrong.
If you think His love would be deeper if your thoughts were,
wrong again.

— 32 —

Nothing comes your way that has not first passed
through the filter of God's love.

"COME TO ME, ALL OF YOU
WHO ARE TIRED AND HAVE HEAVY LOADS,
AND I WILL GIVE YOU REST."

MATTHEW 11:28

— 33 —

Be kind to yourself. God thinks you're worth His kindness.
And He's a good judge of character.

— 34 —

God has plenty of compassion.
He doesn't think your fears are foolish or silly.

— 35 —

You aren't an accident or an incident;
you are a gift to the world, a divine work of art, signed by God.

— 36 —

God can turn any tragedy into a triumph, if only you will
wait and watch.

— 37 —

We need a shepherd.
We need a shepherd to care for us and to guide us.
And we have one.
One who knows us by name.

— 38 —

We don't know what it takes to run the world, and wise are
we who leave the work to God's hands.

— 39 —

God's ways are always right. They may not make sense to us.
But they are right.

— 40 —

Don't think God is listening to your prayers?
Indeed He is. But He may have higher plans.

THE LORD IS MY SHEPHERD;
I HAVE EVERYTHING I NEED.

———

PSALM 23:1

— 41 —

May we have no higher goal than to see someone think
more highly of our Father, our King.

— 42 —

If you were the only person on earth, the earth would look exactly
the same. God would not diminish its beauty one degree
… because He did it all for you.

— 43 —

When you turn to God *for* help, He runs to you *to* help.

— 44 —

God never promises to remove us from our struggles.
He does promise, however, to change the way we look at them.

— 45 —

Long before you knew you needed someone to provide for your needs,
God already had.

— 46 —

No leaf falls without God's knowledge.
No wave crashes on the shore without His calculation.
He has never been surprised.
Not once.

— 47 —

Others may abandon you, divorce you, and ignore you,
but God will love you.
Always.

CHAPTER 2

A *Simple* HOPE

— 48 —

God's help is near and always available,
but it is only given to those who seek it.

— 49 —

Write today's worries in sand. Chisel yesterday's victories in stone.

— 50 —

Life at times appears to fall into pieces, seems irreparable.
But it's going to be okay. How can you know?
Because *God* so loved the world.

— 51 —

Jesus offers a unique-to-Him invitation in which He works and we
trust; He dies and we live; He invites and we believe.

— 52 —

If you want to touch God's heart, use the name He loves to hear.
Call him Father.

— 53 —

Your prayers are honored as precious jewels.
Your words do not stop until they reach the very throne of God.

— 54 —

God doesn't improve; He perfects.
He doesn't enhance; He completes.

— 55 —

Confession is telling God you did the thing He saw you do.
He doesn't need to hear it as much as you need to say it.

— 56 —

Your prayer on earth activates God's power in heaven.

— 57 —

When asked to describe the width of His love, Christ stretched one
hand to the right and the other to the left and had them nailed
in that position so you would know He died loving you.

— 58 —

Allow God's love to change the way you look at you.

— 59 —

Before you go anywhere else with your disappointments, go to God.

*F*AITH MEANS BEING SURE OF THE THINGS
WE HOPE FOR AND KNOWING THAT SOMETHING
IS REAL EVEN IF WE DO NOT SEE IT.

HEBREWS 11:1

*B*EING MADE RIGHT WITH GOD BY HIS GRACE,
WE COULD HAVE THE HOPE OF RECEIVING
THE LIFE THAT NEVER ENDS.

TITUS 3:7

— 60 —

The more hopeless your circumstances,
the more likely your salvation.

— 61 —

Whether you work at home or in the marketplace,
your work matters to God.

— 62 —

Not only is worry irrelevant, accomplishing nothing;
worry is irreverent, distrusting God.

— 63 —

You may feel alone in the wilderness, but you are not.
God is with you.

— 64 —

Your part is prayer and gratitude. God's part? Peace and protection.

— 65 —

God placed His hand on the shoulder of humanity and said,
"You're something special."

— 66 —

Christ came to earth for one reason: to give His life as a ransom
for you, for me, for all of us.
He sacrificed Himself to give us a second chance.

— 67 —

Your prayers move God to change the world.

— 68 —

No one is useless to God. No one.

— 69 —

We are significant, not because of what we do,
but because of whose we are.

— 70 —

Blessed are those who acknowledge that there is only one God
and have quit applying for His position.

— 71 —

Christ responds to universal sin with a universal sacrifice,
taking on the sins of the entire world.

— 72 —

God has proven Himself a faithful Father.
Now it falls to us to be trusting children.

— 73 —

Worship is the "thank you" that refuses to be silenced.

— 74 —

The more we immerse ourselves in grace,
the more likely we are to give grace.

— 75 —

Hope is not a granted wish or a favor performed;
it is far greater than that. It is a zany, unpredictable dependence
on a God who loves to surprise us out of our socks.

— 76 —

You cannot be anything you want to be.
But you can be everything God wants you to be.

— 77 —

Want to worry less? Then pray more. Rather than look forward in fear,
look upward in faith.

— 78 —

The shepherd selects the trail and prepares the pasture.
The sheep's job—our job—is to watch the shepherd.

— 79 —

A little rain can straighten a flower stem.
A little love can change a life.

— 80 —

Our Shepherd majors in restoring hope to the soul.

— 81 —

I've never been surprised by God's judgment,
but I'm still stunned by His grace.

— 82 —

It's not every day that you find someone who will give you a
second chance—much less someone who will give you a
second chance every day. But in Jesus, you find both.

— 83 —

The cost of your sins is more than you can pay.
The gift of your God is more than you can imagine.

Do not worry about anything, but pray and ask God for everything you need, always giving thanks.

PHILIPPIANS 4:6

— 84 —

In every age of history, on every page of Scripture, the truth is revealed: God allows us to make our own choices.

— 85 —

The God-centered life works. And it rescues us from a life that doesn't.

— 86 —

Rather than worry about anything, "pray about everything."

— 87 —

If you're looking for a place with no change, try a soda machine. With life comes change.

— 88 —

What people think of us matters not.
What they think of God matters all.

— 89 —

Your body is God's tool. Maintain it. Your body is God's temple.
Respect it.

— 90 —

You may go days without thinking of God,
but there's never a moment when he's not thinking of you.

— 91 —

We hide. God seeks. We bring sin. He brings a sacrifice.

— 92 —

The purpose of prayer is not to change God but to change us.

— 93 —

God hasn't given up on you.
He hasn't turned away. He believes in you.

— 94 —

All of us are here by grace and, at some point,
all of us have to share some grace.

— 95 —

Christ has changed you from the inside out.
Temptation will pester you, but temptation will not master you.

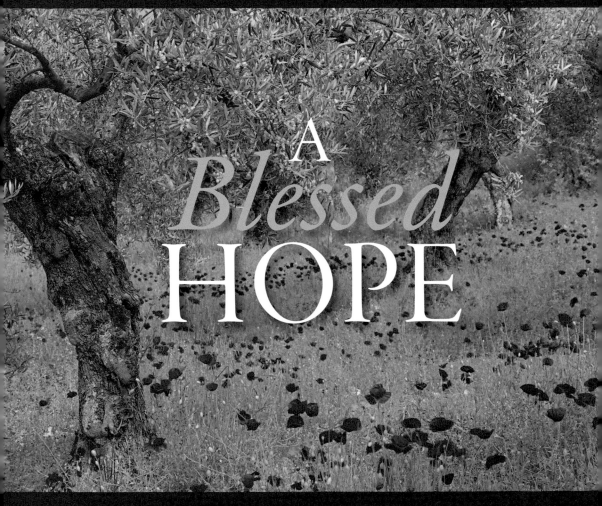

CHAPTER 3

A
Blessed
HOPE

— 96 —

God takes you *however* He finds you. No need to clean up or climb up.
Just look up.

— 97 —

Christ lived the life we could not live and took the punishment
we could not take to offer the hope we cannot resist.

— 98 —

God's goodness is spurred by His nature, not by our worthiness.

— 99 —

With God in you, you have a million resources
that you did not have before!

— 100 —

When all of earth turns against you, all of heaven turns toward you.

— 101 —

The one to whom we pray knows our feelings.
He knows temptation. He has felt discouraged.

— 102 —

What is grace? It's what someone gives us out of the goodness of
His heart, not out of the perfection of ours.

— 103 —

God promises not just peace but perfect peace.
Undiluted, unspotted, unhindered peace.

— 104 —

Catalog God's goodnesses. Meditate on them. He has fed you, led you, and earned your trust. Remember what God has done for you.

— 105 —

The people God used to change history were a ragbag of ne'er-do-wells and has-beens who found hope, not in their performance, but in God's proverbially open arms.

— 106 —

Hell's misery is deep, but not as deep as God's love.

— 107 —

God has sent His angels to care for you, His Holy Spirit to dwell in you, His church to encourage you, and His word to guide you.

*Y*OU, LORD, GIVE TRUE PEACE

TO THOSE WHO DEPEND ON YOU,

BECAUSE THEY TRUST YOU.

———

ISAIAH 26:3

— 108 —

The clothing of Christ on the cross? Sin—yours and mine ... .
He wore our sin so we could wear His righteousness.

— 109 —

God loves you with an unfailing love.

— 110 —

I wonder, how many burdens is Jesus carrying for us
that we know nothing about?

— 111 —

Goodness and mercy follow the child of God each and every day!

— 112 —

For all the things God does do, this is one thing He refuses to do.
He refuses to keep a list of my wrongs.

— 113 —

No struggle will come your way apart from God's purpose,
presence and permission.

— 114 —

He could have lived over us or away from us. But He didn't.
He lived *among* us.
He became a friend of the sinner and brother of the poor.

— 115 —

We are always in the presence of God.
There is never a non-sacred moment!

SURELY GOODNESS AND MERCY

SHALL FOLLOW ME ALL THE DAYS OF MY LIFE;

AND I WILL DWELL IN THE HOUSE OF

THE LORD FOREVER.

———

PSALM 23:6 NKJV

— 116 —

Jesus spent over three decades wading through the muck and mire of our sin yet still saw enough beauty in us to die for our mistakes.

— 117 —

Don't we have *big* problems, *big* worries, *big* questions?
Of course we do.
Hence we need a big view of God.

— 118 —

God's faithfulness has never depended on the faithfulness of His children. He is faithful even when we aren't.

— 119 —

God never gives up.

— 120 —

God sees the worst of you and loves you still. Your sins of tomorrow
and failings of the future will not surprise Him; He sees them now.

— 121 —

Long to be more loving? Begin by accepting your
place as a dearly loved child of God.

— 122 —

Don't measure the size of the mountain;
talk to the One who can move it.

— 123 —

God believes in you enough to call you His ambassador, His follower,
even His child. Why not take His cue and believe in yourself?

*G*LORIFY THE LORD WITH ME,
AND LET US PRAISE HIS NAME TOGETHER.

PSALM 34:3

— 124 —

When you turn to God for help, He runs to you to help. Why?
He knows how you feel.

— 125 —

Want to know the coolest thing about the One who gave up the crown
of heaven for a crown of thorns? He did it for you. Just for you.

— 126 —

Weary of an ordinary existence? The cure for the
common life begins and ends with God.

— 127 —

God has a great race for you to run. Under His care you will go where
you've never been and serve in ways you've never dreamed.

— 128 —

God's grace is older than your sin and greater than your sin.

— 129 —

Who knows the path better than the One who made it? And who
knows the pitfalls of the path better than the One who has walked it?

— 130 —

Our hearts are not large enough to contain the
blessings that God wants to give.

— 131 —

What we want is God. Only when we find Him will we be satisfied.

— 132 —

Yes, God is holy.
Yes, we are sinful.
But, yes, yes, yes, Jesus is our mediator.

— 133 —

When your deepest desire is not the things of God, or a favor from God,
but God Himself, you cross a threshold.

— 134 —

Our convictions tend to change. Good to know God's don't.

— 135 —

Our God is no fair-weather Father.
He's not into this love-'em-and-leave-'em stuff.
You can count on Him to be in your corner no matter how you perform.

THANK THE LORD BECAUSE HE IS GOOD.

HIS LOVE CONTINUES FOREVER.

———

PSALM 106:1

— 136 —

Worship is when you're aware that what you've
been given is far greater than what you can give.

— 137 —

We are all beggars in need of bread, sinners in need of grace,
strugglers in need of strength.

— 138 —

Try shifting your glance away from the one who has hurt you
and settling your eyes on the One who has saved you.

— 139 —

God rewards those who seek *Him*. Not those who seek
doctrine or religion or systems or creeds.

— 140 —

The power of prayer does not depend on the one who makes
the prayer but on the One who hears the prayer.

— 141 —

Think of prayers less as an activity for God
and more as an awareness of God.

— 142 —

When you believe in Christ,
Christ works a miracle in you.

— 143 —

You are who God says you are.
Spiritually alive.
Heavenly positioned.
Connected to the Father.
A billboard of mercy.
An honored child.

CHAPTER 4

A
Pure
HOPE

— 144 —

Christ became one of us. And He did so to redeem all of us.

— 145 —

God will not let you go. He has handcuffed Himself to you in love.
And He owns the only key.

— 146 —

Christ is in you!
Your heart is His home, and He is your master.

— 147 —

God makes healthy what is sick,
right what is wrong, straight what is crooked.

— 148 —

Your eyes see your faults. Your faith sees your Savior.

— 149 —

The blood of Christ does not cover your sins, conceal your sins,
postpone your sins, or diminish your sins.
It takes away your sins, once and for all time.

— 150 —

It's against God's nature to remember forgiven sins.

— 151 —

God loves you simply because He has chosen to do so.

I WILL SING OF THE MERCIES OF THE LORD FOREVER; WITH MY MOUTH WILL I MAKE KNOWN YOUR FAITHFULNESS TO ALL GENERATIONS.

PSALM 89:1 NKJV

— 152 —

The love of God is born from within Him,
not from what He finds in us.

— 153 —

The big news of the Bible is not that you love God
but that God loves you.

— 154 —

Since you are God's idea, you are a good idea.

— 155 —

God is God. He knows what He is doing.
When you can't trace His hand, trust His heart.

— 156 —

You will never be completely happy on earth simply
because you were not made for earth.

— 157 —

God loves you just the way you are, but He refuses to leave you that
way. He wants you to be just like Jesus.

— 158 —

Isn't is good to know that even when we don't love with a perfect love,
God does?

— 159 —

God's lights in our dark nights are as numerous as the stars,
if only we'll look for them.

— 160 —

Within reach of your prayers is the maker of the oceans. God!

— 161 —

Don't ask God to do what you want.
Ask God to do what is right.

— 162 —

You will never forgive anyone more than God has already forgiven you.

— 163 —

I challenge you to find one soul who came to God
seeking grace and did not find it.

*I*f WE LOVE EACH OTHER, GOD LIVES IN US,

AND HIS LOVE IS MADE PERFECT IN US.

———

I JOHN 4:12

— 164 —

Jesus knew that each human being is a treasure. And because He did, people were not a source of stress but a source of joy.

— 165 —

God does what we cannot do so we can be what we dare not dream: perfect before God.

— 166 —

God was ... and is ... Love.
Go to the beginning
of every decision He has made
and you'll find it.
Go to the end of every story He has told
and you'll see it.
Love.

— 167 —

Christ has proven worthy. He has shown that He never fails.
That's what makes God, God.

— 168 —

It's time to let God's love cover all things in your life.
All secrets. All hurts. All hours of evil, minutes of worry.

— 169 —

God lives to hear your heartbeat. He loves to hear your prayers.
He'd die for your sin before He'd let you die in your sin, so He did.

— 170 —

God's hands draw together the disjointed blotches in our
life and render them an expression of His love.

THOSE WHO LIVE IN LOVE

LIVE IN GOD AND

GOD LIVES IN THEM.

———

I JOHN 4:16

— 171 —

The Lord is with us. And, since the Lord is near,
everything is different. Everything!

— 172 —

Many people tell us to love. Only God gives us the power to do so.

— 173 —

God offers authentic love. His devotion is the real deal. But He won't
give you the genuine until you surrender the imitations.

— 174 —

God may not do what you want, but He will do what is right
... and best.

— 175 —

With His own pierced hands, Jesus created a pasture for the soul.
He tore out the thorny underbrush of condemnation.
He pried loose the huge boulders of sin.
In their place He planted seeds of grace and dug ponds of mercy.
And He invites us to rest there.

— 176 —

God does only what is good.

— 177 —

God comes into your world. He comes to do what you can't.

— 178 —

Why doesn't God make you more like Him? He is.
He's just not finished yet.

THE SCRIPTURES GIVE US PATIENCE
AND ENCOURAGEMENT SO THAT
WE CAN HAVE HOPE.

ROMANS 15:4

— 179 —

Every act of heaven reveals God's glory.
Every act of Jesus did the same.

— 180 —

God lets you excel so you can make Him known.

— 181 —

God will use whatever He wants to display His glory. Heavens and
stars. History and nations. People and problems.

— 182 —

To pray "Thy will be done" is to seek the heart of God.

— 183 —

Have you ever been given a gift that compares with God's grace?
Finding this treasure of mercy makes the poorest beggar a prince.

— 184 —

The one who saved your soul longs to remake your heart.
His plan is nothing short of a total transformation.

— 185 —

Does God love us because of our goodness?
No, He loves us because of His goodness.

— 186 —

We live beneath the protective palm of a sovereign King
who superintends every circumstance of our lives
and delights in doing us good.

WE KNOW THAT IN EVERYTHING
GOD WORKS FOR THE GOOD OF
THOSE WHO LOVE HIM.

ROMANS 8:28

— 187 —

God loves you.
Personally.
Powerfully.
Passionately.

— 188 —

Jesus had kindness for the diseased and
mercy for the rebellious
and courage for the challenges.
God wants you to have the same.

— 189 —

The greatest discovery in the universe is
the greatest love in the universe—
God's love.

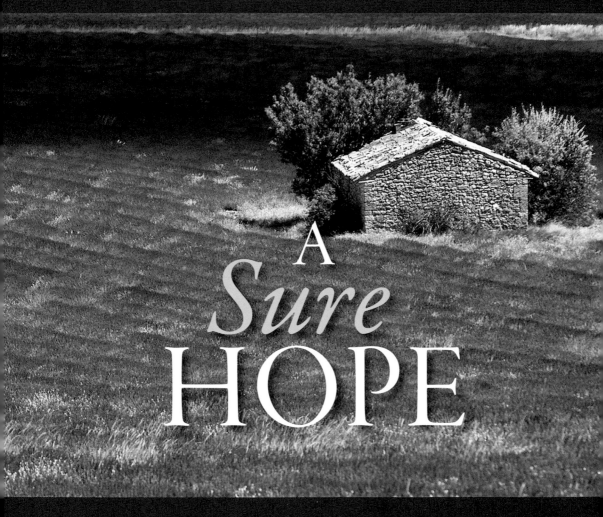

CHAPTER 5

A
Sure
HOPE

— 190 —

God is never too late or too early, too fast or too slow.
He has always been and always will be right.

— 191 —

Our devotion may falter, but God's never does.

— 192 —

God is leading you.
Leave tomorrow's problems until tomorrow.

— 193 —

God loves you when you don't feel lovely.
He loves you when no one else loves you.

— 194 —

God designed you. And His design defines your destiny.

— 195 —

God's hope pours into your world.
Upon the sick, He shines the ray of healing.
To the bereaved, He gives the promise of reunion.
To the confused, He offers the light of Scripture.

— 196 —

The amount of the check is "sufficient grace."
The signer of the check is Jesus.

— 197 —

God does more than forgive our mistakes; He removes them!
We simply have to take them to Him.

Patience produces character, and character produces hope. And this hope will never disappoint us.

ROMANS 5:4-5

— 198 —

Next time you're disappointed, don't panic. Don't give up.
Just be patient and let God remind you He's still in control.

— 199 —

Focus on giants—you stumble.
Focus on God—your giants tumble.

— 200 —

When the first angel lifted the first wing,
God had already always been.

— 201 —

The cross. Strange that a tool of torture would
come to embody a movement of hope.

— 202 —

Christ's resurrection is an exploding flare announcing
to all sincere seekers that it is safe to believe.

— 203 —

We must trust God. We must trust not only that
He does what is best but that He knows what is ahead.

— 204 —

Our God is not aloof—He's not so far above us that He can't see
and understand our problems. He's a Savior who came down
and lived and worked with the people.

— 205 —

We are welcome to enter into God's presence—any day, any time.

— 206 —

Jesus tends to His sheep. And He will tend to you.

— 207 —

If God is able to place the stars in their sockets
and suspend the sky like a curtain,
do you think it remotely possible that He is able to guide your life?

— 208 —

Our mood may shift, but God's doesn't.
Our devotion may falter, but God's never does.

— 209 —

Honestly, now. Did God save you so you would fret?
Would He teach you to walk just to watch you fall?
Would He be nailed to the cross for your sins and then
disregard your prayers? I don't think so.

I HAVE GOOD PLANS FOR YOU,

NOT PLANS TO HURT YOU.

I WILL GIVE YOU HOPE AND A GOOD FUTURE.

———

JEREMIAH 29:11

— 210 —

If something is important to you, it's important to God.

— 211 —

Nails didn't hold God to a cross. Love did.

— 212 —

Your parents may have given you genes, but God gives you grace.
Your parents may be responsible for your body,
but God has taken charge of your soul.

— 213 —

God has never taken His eyes off you. Not for a millisecond.
He's always near.

— 214 —

God's thoughts of you outnumber the sand on the shore.
You never leave His mind, escape His sight, flee His thoughts.

— 215 —

The God who ruled the earth last night is the same God
who rules it today. Same convictions. Same plan.
Same mood. Same love. He never changes.

— 216 —

What frightens us does not frighten God.
What troubles us does not trouble Him.

— 217 —

Whatever you are facing, God knows how you feel.

With men this is impossible,
but with God all things are possible.

MATTHEW 19:26 NKJV

— 218 —

We have a Father who is at His best when we are at our worst.
A Father whose grace is strongest when our devotion is weakest.

— 219 —

If you have the Shepherd, you have grace for every sin,
direction for every turn, a candle for every corner, and an
anchor for every storm. You have everything you need.

— 220 —

Need unchanging truth to trust? Try God's. His truth never wavers.

— 221 —

Do yourself a favor; take your anxious moments to the cross.
Leave them there with your bad moments and your mad moments.

— 222 —

You can trust God. He has given His love to you;
why don't you give your doubts to Him?

— 223 —

God keeps his promise. See for yourself. In the manger. He's there.
See for yourself. In the tomb. He's gone.

— 224 —

Nothing is concealed from God.
He is all-powerful, all-knowing, and all-present.

— 225 —

Salvation is God-given, God-driven, God-empowered, and
God-originated. The gift is not from man to God. It is from God to man.

— 226 —

God is as near to us on Monday as on Sunday.
In the school room as in the sanctuary.

— 227 —

God is not the God of confusion, and wherever He sees sincere
seekers with confused hearts, you can bet your sweet December
He will do whatever it takes to help them see His will.

— 228 —

Ask God for whatever you need. He is committed to you.

— 229 —

God's salvation song has two verses. He not only took
your place on the cross; He takes His place in your heart.

*I*T IS BY GRACE YOU HAVE BEEN SAVED,

THROUGH FAITH—

AND THIS NOT FROM YOURSELVES,

IT IS THE GIFT OF GOD—NOT BY WORKS,

SO THAT NO ONE CAN BOAST.

———

EPHESIANS 2:8-9 NIV

— 230 —

When you accept Christ, God seals you with His Holy Spirit.
He paid too high a price to leave you unguarded.

— 231 —

To the lonely, Jesus whispers, "I've been there."
To the discouraged, Christ nods His head and sighs, "I've been there."

— 232 —

God is constantly and aggressively communicating with the world
through His word. God is still speaking!

— 233 —

Having trouble putting up with ungrateful relatives or cranky neigh-
bors? God puts up with you when you act the same.

— 234 —

God knows your entire story,
from first word to final breath,
and with clear assessment declares,
"You are mine."

$\mathcal{N}$OTHING ABOVE US,
NOTHING BELOW US, NOR
ANYTHING ELSE IN THE WHOLE WORLD
WILL EVER BE ABLE TO
SEPARATE US FROM THE
LOVE OF GOD THAT
IS IN CHRIST JESUS OUR LORD.

ROMANS 8:39

CHAPTER 6

A *Vital* HOPE

— 235 —

When Jesus says He will keep you safe, He means it.

— 236 —

Jesus says He is the solution for weariness of soul.

— 237 —

You can talk to God because God listens.
Your voice matters in heaven.

— 238 —

You need not win God's love. You already have it.
And, since you can't win it, you can't lose it.

— 239 —

God wants you to fly. He wants you to fly free of yesterday's guilt.
He wants you to fly free of today's fears.
He wants you to fly free of tomorrow's grave.

— 240 —

"He restores my soul," wrote the shepherd.
He doesn't reform; He restores. He doesn't camouflage the old;
He restores the new. He will restore the hope. He will restore the soul.

— 241 —

You can bet that He who made you
knows just how to purify you—from the inside out.

— 242 —

If God cares enough about the planet Saturn to give it rings …
is there an outside chance that He cares enough
about you to meet your needs?

— 243 —

Your goodness can't win God's love. Nor can your badness lose it.
But you can resist it.

— 244 —

One good choice for eternity offsets a thousand bad ones on earth.
The choice is yours.

— 245 —

God looked at your entire life, determined your assignment,
and gave you the tools to do the job.

*H*e restores my soul;

HE LEADS ME IN THE PATHS OF RIGHTEOUSNESS

FOR HIS NAME'S SAKE.

———

PSALM 23:3 NKJV

GOD SO LOVED THE WORLD
THAT HE GAVE HIS ONLY BEGOTTEN SON THAT
WHOEVER BELIEVES IN HIM SHOULD NOT PERISH
BUT HAVE EVERLASTING LIFE.

JOHN 3:16 NKJV

— 246 —

The heart of the human problem is the heart of the human.
And God's treatment is prescribed in John 3:16.
He loves. He gives. We believe. We live.

— 247 —

God has involved Himself in the carpools, heartbreaks,
and funeral homes of our day.

— 248 —

Don't quit.
For if you do, you may miss the answer to your prayers.

— 249 —

With God there are no accidents.
Every incident is intended to bring us closer to Him.

— 250 —

God is using today's difficulties to strengthen you for tomorrow.

— 251 —

Our Savior kneels down and gazes upon the darkest acts of our lives.
But rather than recoil in horror, He reaches out in kindness and says,
"I can clean that if you want."

— 252 —

God made you *you-nique*.

— 253 —

In the great orchestra we call life, you have an instrument and a song,
and you owe it to God to play them both sublimely.

— 254 —

The past you cannot change, but your response to your past you can.

— 255 —

For all its peculiarities and unevenness, the Bible has a simple story.
God made man. Man rejected God.
God won't give up until He wins him back.

— 256 —

God honors radical, risk-taking faith.

— 257 —

Worship is the awareness that were it not for God's touch,
you'd still be hobbling and hurting, bitter and broken.

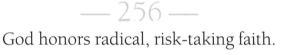

THE BLOOD OF JESUS, GOD'S SON,

CLEANSES US FROM EVERY SIN.

I JOHN 1:7

— 258 —

Your body is God's instrument,
intended for His work and for His glory.

— 259 —

You can do something no one else can do in a fashion
no one else can do it. When you do the most what you do the best,
you put a smile on God's face.

— 260 —

What prayer does is invite God to walk
the shadowy pathways of life with us.

— 261 —

God can lead you into a worry-free world. Be quick to pray.
Focus less on the problems ahead and more on the victories behind.

*L*ET YOUR REQUESTS BE MADE KNOWN
TO GOD; AND THE PEACE OF GOD,
WHICH SURPASSES ALL UNDERSTANDING, WILL
GUARD YOUR HEARTS AND MINDS
THROUGH CHRIST JESUS.

PHILIPPIANS 4:6-7 NKJV

When you know God loves you,
you won't be desperate for the love of others.

God has not asked us to settle the score or get even. Ever.

God doesn't give laws for our pleasure.
He gives them for our protection.

— 265 —

Prior to creation the universe was not a dark space.
The universe did not exist.

— 266 —

Rather than begrudge your problem, explore it. Ponder it.
And most of all, use it. Use it to the glory of God.

— 267 —

You may be willing to stop being God's child.
But God is not willing to stop being your Father.

— 268 —

The key to knowing God's heart is having a relationship with Him.
A *personal* relationship.

— 269 —

God is committed to caring for our needs.
Our provision is His priority.

DEPEND ON THE LORD;

TRUST HIM, AND HE WILL

TAKE CARE OF YOU.

PSALM 37:5

— 270 —

Just as unconfessed sin hinders joy, confessed sin releases it.

— 271 —

Regardless of the circumstances that surrounded your arrival,
you are not an accident. God planned you before you were born.

— 272 —

Welcome Christ into the inner workings of your life.
Let Him be the water of your soul.

— 273 —

The greatest force in the cosmos understands and
intercedes for you.

— 274 —

You are saved, not because of what you do,
but because of what Christ did.

— 275 —

With perfect knowledge of the past and perfect vision of the future,
God loves you perfectly in spite of both.

— 276 —

God knows you.
He keeps your tears in a bottle.
He knows you.
He is near you.

*Y*OU NUMBER MY WANDERINGS;
PUT MY TEARS INTO YOUR BOTTLE.

———

PSALM 56:8 NKJV

CHAPTER 7

AN *Eternal* HOPE

— 277 —

God honors us with the freedom to choose where we spend eternity.

— 278 —

God invites us to love Him. He urges us to love Him.
But, in the end, the choice is yours and mine.

— 279

If God must choose between your earthly satisfaction and
your heavenly salvation, which do you hope He chooses?
Me too.

— 280 —

Heaven is populated by those who let God change them.
Every sin is gone. Every insecurity is forgotten. Every fear is past.
Pure love. No lust. Pure hope. No fear.

— 281 —

God is not just alive, but life itself.
God never began and will never cease. He exists endlessly, always.

— 282 —

God may speak through nature or nurture, majesty, or mishap.
But through all and to all He invites: "Come, enjoy Me forever."

— 283 —

Answer the big question of eternity,
and the little questions of life fall into perspective.

— 284 —

God never said that the journey would be easy,
but He did say that the arrival would be worthwhile.

— 285 —

He stilled a storm with one command. He raised the dead with one proclamation. He rerouted the history of the world with one life.

— 286 —

God has always been and always will be right. He is righteous.

— 287 —

When it comes to describing heaven, we are all happy failures.

— 288 —

God is not a miser with His grace.

— 289 —

The Land of Promise, says Jesus, awaits those who endure.

— 290 —

On the eve of the cross, Jesus made His decision.
He would rather go to hell for you than go to heaven without you.

— 291 —

God loves you with an everlasting love.

— 292 —

Through Christ's sacrifice, our past is pardoned and our future secure.

— 293 —

Of all the blessings of heaven, one of the greatest will be you!
You will be God's magnum opus, His work of art. The angels will gasp.
God's work will be completed. At last, you will have a heart like His.

— 294 —

How could a loving God send people to hell? He doesn't.
He simply honors the choice of sinners.

— 295 —

Please understand. God's goal is not to make you happy.
His goal is to make you His. His goal is not to get you what you want;
it is to get you what you need.

*I*F WE ARE NOT FAITHFUL,

HE WILL STILL BE FAITHFUL,

BECAUSE HE CANNOT BE FALSE TO HIMSELF.

———

2 TIMOTHY 2:13

— 296 —

God's highest dream is not to make us rich, not to make us successful
or popular or famous. God's dream is to make us right with Him.

— 297 —

God's blessings are dispensed according to the riches of His grace,
not according to the depth of our faith.

— 298 —

God's greatest creation is not the flung stars or the gorged canyons;
it's His eternal plan to reach His children.

— 299 —

Do you feel a need for affirmation? You need only pause at the base
of the cross and be reminded of this: The Maker of the stars would
rather die for you than live without you. And that is a fact.

— 300 —

God does not change. He is the "I am" God.

— 301 —

To behold Christ is to become like Him.
As He dominates your thoughts, He changes you from one degree of
glory to another until—hang on!—you are ready to live with Him.

— 302 —

Jesus allows your mistakes to be lost in His perfection.

— 303 —

Someday God will wipe away your tears.
The hands that stretched the heavens will touch your cheeks.
The hands that curled in agony as the Roman spike cut through
will someday cup your face and brush away your tears. Forever.

— 304 —

When Jesus went home he left the front door open.

— 305 —

You cannot control the way your forefathers responded to God.
But you can control the way you respond to him.

— 306 —

God knows your beginning and your end because he has neither.

— 307 —

Place your mistake before the judgment seat of God.
Let Him condemn it, let Him pardon it, and put it away.

LET US HOLD FIRMLY TO THE HOPE THAT WE HAVE CONFESSED, BECAUSE WE CAN TRUST GOD TO DO WHAT HE PROMISED.

HEBREWS 10:23

— 308 —
God's strength never diminishes.
Yours and mine will and has.

— 309 —
As heaven's advertising agency, we promote God in every area of life.

— 310 —
Your eternal salvation and your evening meal come
from the same hand.

— 311 —
Would we love as God loves?
Then we start by receiving God's love.

— 312 —

One of the supreme promises of God is simply this:
if you have given your life to Jesus, Jesus has given Himself to you.
He has made your heart His home.

— 313 —

Our awareness of God's presence may falter,
but the reality of His presence never changes.

— 314 —

You hang as God's work of art, a testimony in His gallery of grace.

— 315 —

In heaven the winner's circle isn't reserved for a handful of the elite,
but for a heaven full of God's children.

— 316 —

Receive God's hope, won't you?
Receive it because you need it.
Receive it so you can share it.

ACKNOWLEDGEMENTS

Grateful acknowledgement is made to the following publishers for permission to reprint this copyrighted material. All copyrights are held by the author, Max Lucado. (Quotes are listed by number.)

The Applause of Heaven (Nashville: Word, 1990).
[17, 21, 66, 240, 253, 283, 303]

In the Eye of the Storm (Nashville: Word, 1991).
[54, 70, 73, 98, 136, 159, 164, 166, 174, 257, 279, 284]

He Still Moves Stones (Nashville: Word, 1993).
[6, 48, 60, 72, 177, 198, 210, 248, 256]

When God Whispers Your Name (Nashville: Word, 1994).
[23, 55, 68, 81, 131, 148, 149, 156, 161, 162, 163, 211, 212, 223, 236, 254, 263, 287, 304, 305]

The Inspirational Study Bible (Nashville: W Publishing Group, 1995).
[27, 102, 155, 204]

A Gentle Thunder (Nashville: Word, 1995).
[18, 19, 25, 37, 118, 167, 203, 235, 249, 250, 255, 297]

In the Grip of Grace (Nashville: Word, 1996).
[35, 65, 69, 74, 83, 128, 160, 165, 178, 209, 225, 264, 292, 296]

The Great House of God (Nashville: Word, 1997).
[8, 31, 42, 45, 52, 53, 56, 67, 90, 92, 94, 135, 137, 140, 146, 182, 184, 207, 216, 226, 227, 228, 237, 242, 267, 268, 269, 270, 310]

Just Like Jesus (Nashville: Word, 1998).
[5, 10, 11, 44, 58, 115, 116, 117, 138, 139, 157, 184, 188, 251, 271, 280, 293, 312, 313]

When Christ Comes (Nashville: Word, 1999).
[14, 106, 107, 114, 202, 294, 315]

Traveling Light (Nashville: W Publishing Group, 2000).
[15, 30, 34, 59, 63, 78, 80, 111, 122, 127, 129, 130, 171, 175, 176, 190, 191, 192, 195, 206, 208, 215, 219, 222, 262, 286, 288, 299]

He Chose the Nails (Nashville: W Publishing Group, 2000).
[3, 9, 36, 57, 84, 108, 125, 132, 197, 201, 205, 221, 244]

A Love Worth Giving (Nashville: W Publishing Group, 2002).
[20, 29, 33, 47, 79, 91, 93, 109, 121, 123, 151, 152, 158, 168, 172, 185, 187, 193, 233, 241, 274, 302, 311, 316]

And the Angels Were Silent (Nashville: W Publishing Group, 2003).
[22, 100, 239, 247, 277, 278, 285, 290, 298]

God Came Near (Nashville: W Publishing Group, 2003).
[75, 112, 150]

Next Door Savior (Nashville: W Publishing Group, 2003).
[16, 43, 95, 99, 110, 124, 142, 196, 217, 231, 232, 273, 300, 301]

No Wonder They Call Him the Savior (Nashville: W Publishing Group, 2003).
[2, 12, 82, 101, 105, 260, 289]

Six Hours One Friday (Nashville: W Publishing Group, 2003).
[119, 218]

Come Thirsty (Nashville: W Publishing Group, 2004).
[4, 26, 28, 32, 39, 46, 62, 64, 71, 77, 86, 113, 120, 141, 143, 153, 170, 173, 186, 189, 214, 229, 230, 234, 261, 272, 275, 291, 314]

Cure for the Common Life (Nashville: W Publishing Group, 2005).
[1, 24, 61, 76, 126, 154, 169, 194, 213, 245, 252, 259, 276]

It's Not About Me (Nashville: Integrity, 2006).
[38, 40, 41, 85, 87, 88, 89, 133, 134, 179, 180, 181, 220, 224, 258, 265, 266, 306, 308, 309]

Facing Your Giants (Nashville: W Publishing Group, 2006).
[49, 97, 103, 144, 199, 307]

3:16, Numbers of Hope (Nashville: W Publishing Group, 2007).
[7, 13, 50, 51, 96, 104, 145, 147, 200, 238, 243, 246, 281, 282]

MAX LUCADO, Minister of Writing and Preaching for the Oak Hills Church in San Antonio, Texas, is the husband of Denalyn and father of Jenna, Andrea, and Sara. On a good week he reads a good book, has a few dinners with his wife, and breaks 90 on the golf course. He usually settles for the first two.

To SHARE HOW THIS BOOK has
encouraged you or someone close to you,
send us an email at: *feedback@simpletruths.com*

To read more heartfelt stories, view life-inspiring
movies, enjoy daily devotionals, quotes and
Scriptures to strengthen and inspire your faith—
and to share with a friend—visit us at
www.simpletruths.com

simple truths®
Motivational & Inspirational Gifts